Pebble™

Wetland Animals

Herons

great blue heron

by Margaret Hall

Consulting Editor: Gail Saunders-Smith, Ph.D.
Consultant: Charlie Luthin, Executive Director
Wisconsin Wetlands Association, Madison, Wisconsin

Capstone
press

Mankato, Minnesota

Pebble Books are published by Capstone Press
151 Good Counsel Drive, P.O. Box 669, Mankato, Minnesota 56002
http://www.capstonepress.com

1 2 3 4 5 6 09 08 07 06 05 04

Library of Congress Cataloging-in-Publication Data
Hall, Margaret, 1947–
    Herons/by Margaret Hall.
    p. cm.—(Wetland animals)
    Summary: Photographs and simple text introduce the characteristics and
behavior of herons.
    Includes bibliographical references and index.
    ISBN 0-7368-2064-7 (hardcover)
    ISBN 13: 978-0-7368-9492-0 (softcover pbk.)
    ISBN 10: 0-7368-9492-6 (softcover pbk.)
    1. Herons—Juvenile literature. [1. Herons.] I. Title. II. Series.
QL696.C52 H33 2004
598.3′4—dc21   2003008553

Note to Parents and Teachers

The Wetland Animals series supports national science standards
related to life science. This book describes and illustrates herons.
The photographs support early readers in understanding the text.
The repetition of words and phrases helps early readers learn new
words. This book also introduces early readers to subject-specific
vocabulary words, which are defined in the Glossary section. Early
readers may need assistance to read some words and to use the
Table of Contents, Glossary, Read More, Internet Sites, and Index/
Word List sections of the book.

Table of Contents

Herons 5

Wetlands 9

What Herons Do 11

Day and Night 21

Glossary 22

Read More 23

Internet Sites 23

Index/Word List 24

Herons

Herons are birds with long, sharp bills.

blue heron

Herons have white, brown, gray, or green feathers.

goliath heron

places where herons live

8

Wetlands

Herons live around the world. Many herons live in wetlands. Wetlands are areas of land covered by water and plants.

great blue heron

What Herons Do

Herons wade in the water. They do not swim.

little blue heron

Herons stand very still.
Some herons stand on
one leg.

great blue heron

Herons lunge into the water. Herons catch fish with their bills.

black crowned night heron

15

Herons eat crabs, fish, and other water animals. They also eat insects, frogs, and snakes.

yellow crowned night heron

Herons build nests in tall trees. They often roost in colonies with other birds.

great blue heron

Day and Night

Herons eat during the day. They sleep standing in water at night.

snowy egret
(member of the heron family)

Glossary

bill—the hard part of a bird's mouth; a heron uses its bill to catch food.

colony—a large group of birds that build nests near each other

feather—a light, fluffy part that covers a bird's body; heron feathers are waterproof.

lunge—to move forward quickly and suddenly

nest—a home that birds build out of sticks and grass; birds lay their eggs and raise their young in nests.

roost—to settle in a group to rest; some herons roost at night.

wade—to walk in water that is not deep

wetland—an area of land covered by water and plants; marshes, swamps, and bogs are wetlands.

Read More

Donovan, Sandra. *Animals of Rivers, Lakes, and Ponds.* Animals of the Biomes. Austin, Texas: Raintree Steck-Vaughn, 2002.

Kalman, Bobbie, and Amanda Bishop. *What Are Wetlands?* The Science of Living Things. New York: Crabtree, 2003.

Miller, Sara Swan. *Wading Birds: From Herons to Hammerkops.* Animals in Order. New York: Franklin Watts, 2001.

Internet Sites

FactHound offers a safe, fun way to find Internet sites related to this book. All of the sites on FactHound have been researched by our staff.

Here's how:
1. Visit *www.facthound.com*
2. Type in this special code **0736820647** for age-appropriate sites. Or enter a search word related to this book for a more general search.
3. Click on the Fetch It button.

FactHound will fetch the best sites for you!

Index/Word List

bills, 5, 15
birds, 5, 19
build, 19
catch, 15
colonies, 19
day, 21
eat, 17, 21
feathers, 7

fish, 15, 17
leg, 13
live, 9
long, 5
lunge, 15
nests, 19
night, 21
plants, 9

roost, 19
sharp, 5
sleep, 21
stand, 13, 21
still, 13
swim, 11
wade, 11
wetlands, 9

Word Count: 106
Early-Intervention Level: 13

Editorial Credits
Sarah L. Schuette, editor; Patrick D. Dentinger, series designer; Scott Thoms,
    photo researcher; Karen Risch, product planning editor

Photo Credits
Corbis, 12
Corel, 18
Eda Rogers, 14
Houserstock/Dave G. Houser, cover, 1, 8
Lynn M. Stone, 16, 20
Norvia Behling, 10
PhotoDisc Inc., 4, 6